Let in the Sun

Opening your life to God's blessings

By

Daniel Dechenaux

ISBN: 978-1-4033-9122-3 (sc)
ISBN: 978-1-4033-9121-6 (e)

Print information available on the last page.

This book is printed on acid-free paper.

1stBooks – rev. 11/09/2023

Dedicated

with love

to my mother.

TABLE OF CONTENTS

INTRODUCTION

What have you noticed today?

The Lord has provided so many gifts in our world. Each day, perhaps you take some time to see them, to hear them, to feel them, and to taste them. Within these pages are some of these blessings that I have found. What better way to celebrate them than through verse and rhyme? They are brought together in the hope that they will encourage you to find more. To help us find these blessings, the Lord has given us the sun. And the sun, like the Lord, is always with us, even though we might not always be able to see it.

SECTION ONE:

LET IN THE SUN

Daniel Dechenaux

LET IN THE SUN

Early this morning

we opened our eyes

A new day was dawning

filled with surprise

There's so many wonderful

things to be done

So open your window

and let in the sun…

Daniel Dechenaux

WHAT HAVE YOU NOTICED TODAY

Tell me, what have you noticed today,

of the wonders the Lord has displayed?

As you're travelling through

have you found something new?

Tell me, what have you noticed today?

Did you notice the dew on the leaves,

as they sparkled like big diamond rings?

Did you walk by the sea

as the turtles ran free?

Is that what you noticed today?

Did the lightning bugs light up your night?

Did the crickets all creak with delight?

Did you stop to say hi

as the beetle crawled by?

Is that what you noticed today?

LORD

Lord, now that You've come to me,

I can feel all that You've done for me

Lord, You were the only one

To lead me to myself

Like a storm, suddenly at its end

A restless sea, suddenly calm again

A life, that's suddenly born again

Lord, You've done for me

Now I know, that I've been but part of me,

I'm so amazed, how you brought the start of me

Lord, I can do anything, this I now believe

I have my Lord

Daniel Dechenaux

THREE THOUSAND VOICES

(For those we lost on September 11)

Three thousand voices

up in the sky,

Telling us, yes, they're alright

Where did they go?

Why did they go?

Do they know we miss them so?

Three thousand hearts

all waiting there,

Looking down, they see we care

Where did they go?

Why did they go?

Do they know we miss them so?

There's a distant place

where they all await,

and some day we all can go

They will laugh with us,

and they will smile with us,

I believe it will be so

Three thousand dreams

left unfulfilled,

we remember each of them still

When we see them,

we'll surely tell them,

just because they ought to know

SURELY

Surely, the climb will be treacherous

Surely, some rocks will fall

Surely, the clouds will be many

Surely, the wind will blow strong

Surely, there will be doubters

Surely, I'll have regrets

Surely, I'll tumble over

But surely, I will get up

For surely, the sky will be clearing

And surely, the pain will subside

And surely, the wind will stop blowing

And surely, I will arrive

Daniel Dechenaux

MOONLIGHT DANCING

Moonlight dancing, through my curtain

as the cars pass slowly by,

as the rain is softly falling

and the Lord is at my side

Quiet fields of green and yellow

underneath the clear blue sky,

not a sole on the horizon

but the Lord is at my side

Once I wondered why,

every day and night,

what these moments really mean?

When we are alone,

we are not alone,

this was life's true mystery

Standing at the gates of heaven,

there it all comes clear to me,

Daniel Dechenaux

By myself, yet with my maker,

once again, the Lord and me

FROST

Frost, dripping from the sky

onto the towns and the countryside

in the morning

Frost, on the window panes

and the cars that lay

buried in the snow

Daniel Dechenaux

Frost, on an empty church

with a bell that rings

and the people come

Frost, where the children play

with their skates and sleighs

laughing loudly

Frost, will lick your nose

and bite your toes

like a puppy

Frost, God's breath of freshness

onto the world

Daniel Dechenaux

DRIPPITY DROP

Drippity drip, drippity drop

and the rain falls on my roof

Drippity drip, drippity drop,

drippity, drippity, drippity drop

Bibbidy boom, bibbidy boom

and the thunder beats like a drum

Bibbidy boom, bibbidy boom

bibbidy, bibbidy, bibbidy boom

Crickity crick, crickity crack

and the lightning goes like that

Crickity crick, crickity crack

crickity, crickity, crickity crack

I'm not afraid, no I'm not afraid

for the Lord looks over me

I'm not afraid, no I'm not afraid

for the Lord looks over me

Daniel Dechenaux

SHARING

If I may know you

for only awhile

Let me share with you

and make you smile

If we're together

for only today

Let me share with you

and be on my way

Sharing brings sunlight

into the morning,

Sharing brings waves

up to the shore

Sharing brings hearts

closer together,

And all the joy

we're living for

Daniel Dechenaux

THE FOUNTAIN IN THE PARK

I love the fountain in the park

they light it up long after dark

Up and down the water flows

just as life usually goes

Pretty colors, blue and green

such a sight I've never seen

And the children all adore them

as they play and sing their songs

Water dancing in the breeze

like the branches on the trees

Like a lovely ballerina

dancing just for you and me

Swaying left and swaying right

swirling 'round and 'round and 'round

Climbing high, up toward heaven

returning safely to the ground

I love the fountain in the park

they light it up long after dark

Up and down the water flows

just as life usually goes

SOUNDS OF GOODNESS

I hear sounds of goodness

in the purr of a kitten

in the chirp of a robin

in the buzz of the bees

I adore sounds of goodness

early in the morning

as if Nature were performing

especially for me

I hear sounds of goodness

as the seagulls are screaming

as the children are laughing

as the waves swoosh to shore

I adore sounds of goodness

wherever I find them,

and each day I take some time

to listen for more

Daniel Dechenaux

THE TRAIN IN THE NIGHT

I hear a train pass in the night

as the world lies quiet and still

Its whistle calls me, like a friend

inviting me to come along

I wonder where the train would take me

if I should run and jump inside,

what adventures would await me

how many secrets might I find?

We would curl around a mountain,

through an old, abandoned mine,

through a cold and creepy ghost town,

where ghosts play cards and drink their wine

Through a dark, medieval forest

with knights who joust and duel with swords,

through a harbor filled with pirates

hoisting treasure up aboard

Through a deep, majestic canyon

across a quiet country stream,

through a field adorned with daisies

across a bridge into my dreams

The whistle fades into the distance

my heavy eyes begin to close,

when the whistle calls tomorrow

I wonder where my heart will go?

ONE MORE CHANCE

One more ball aglow in yellow

rolling through a sky of blue,

one more day brings one more chance

A chance to taste your favorite food

a chance to hear your favorite song

a chance to laugh and sing

A chance to teach a child

a chance to help a friend

a chance to pursue your dreams

A chance to visit your special places

a chance to visit those close to your heart

a chance to find yourself

One more day brings one more chance

a chance to say, "I'm sorry"

a chance to say, "I love you"

BARBECUE CHICKEN

There's nothin' could ever keep me kickin'

like a big plate of barbecue chicken,

With sauce as sweet as candy and honey

there's no better way to spend my money

Cornbread and beans, a portion of greens

I might as well be inside of a dream

Pass me a piece of potato pie

and I'll come back till the day I die

'Cause there's nothin' could ever keep me

kickin'

like a big plate of barbecue chicken

SECTION TWO:

IT'S A MIRACLE

Daniel Dechenaux

IT'S A MIRACLE

It's a miracle, inside a manger,

underneath a shining star

It's a miracle, inside a manger,

that put love inside our hearts

What is love, if it's not giving

an only begotten son?

What is love, if it's not dying

on a cross for what we've done?

What is love, if not the answer

to our pain and to our strife?

What is love, if not the granting

of a peaceful, eternal life?

It's a miracle, inside a manger,

underneath a shining star

It's a miracle, inside a manger

that put love inside our hearts

Daniel Dechenaux

THE PILLOW BENEATH OUR HEADS

David saw Goliath fall

slew that giant ten feet tall,

But before, he saw it all

with the pillow beneath his head

Harriet saw the slaves go free

Susan saw equality

But they saw it first, you see

with the pillow beneath their heads

Christopher found an uncharted land

Jesse ran passed every man

Just how did they devise these plans?

With the pillow beneath their heads

Now it's up to you and me

as we lie down on our beds

What is it that we can see

with the pillow beneath our heads?

Daniel Dechenaux

JOY

Joy, like the morning sun

lifts our hearts up toward heaven

Joy, like a singer's song

screams out for all to hear

Joy, like an eagle in flight

soars high above the canyon

Joy, like a passing stream

trickles softly through the stones

Joy, like a poet's rhyme

dances in time to be remembered

Joy, like a fury coat

surrounds us to keep us warm

Joy, like the setting sun, returns

to lift our hearts again

SO MUCH MORE

A table carved of nails and wood

with legs as sturdy as he could

His love was always understood

and that was so much more

The smell of boiling spaghetti sauce

a plate of noodles for each of us

Her love was always clear to us

and that was so much more

They had no riches to bestow

not one piece of shining gold

But we had a happy home

and that was so much more

So much more

WATCHIN' THE WORLD GO 'ROUND

Sittin' in the shade

sippin' on my lemonade

thinkin' how I got it made

watchin' the world go 'round

Sailboats passing by

seagulls hanging way up high

surfers twisting in the tide

just watchin' the world go 'round

And the sun is melting lemon drops

right before my eyes

ooey, gooey, chewy lemon drops

falling from the sky

Sittin' in the shade

sippin' on my lemonade

thinkin' how I got it made

watchin' the world go 'round

A LIGHTHOUSE IN A STORM

I believe in you, I believe in me

and in all that we can be

With a spirit there to guide us

like a lighthouse in a storm

I believe in faith, I believe in love

and that will be enough

With a spirit there to guide us

like a lighthouse in a storm

Like a lighthouse in a storm

lead us through the fog

protect us from the evil and the harm

Like a lighthouse in a storm

lead us through the fog

take us to a place that's safe and warm

WALK WITH ME

And my past shall lay before me

as I stand alone with Thee

Grant me everlasting glory

walk with me across the sea

Harbor lights that shine so brightly

reveal the perils that lie beneath

Let me wade in Your redemption

walk with me across the sea

Walk with me and make me holy

walk with me and set me free

Walk with me and make me holy

walk with me across the sea

FREE

Free, as the butterflies

floating high above the meadow

Free, as the bumblebees

around the trees and in the nectar

Free, as the waterfall

splashing down onto the river

Free, as the summer breeze

caressing our cheeks

Free, as the cotton clouds

drifting under heaven

Free, as a caring heart

sharing sparks of imagination

Free, for God to see

as surely He meant us to be

SECTION THREE:

A BETTER PLACE

Daniel Dechenaux

A BETTER PLACE

I knew a man of no disgrace

he had a mustache on his face

one day he quit the human race

to try and find a better place

He ventured to a vacant lot

moved into a cardboard box

watched the holes grow in his sox

and he dreamed of a better place

There he sat through cold and rain

heavy winds and hurricanes

never once did he complain

but he dreamed of a better place

A little boy came walking by

saw him there and asked him why,

"Don't you worry, I'll get by,

I'm going to a better place."

At last, he smiled and closed his eyes,

unafraid of his time to die,

he scratched the mustache on his face

and went into a better place

Daniel Dechenaux

THE MODEL KIT

I found a hundred dollar bill

beneath my bedroom window sill

and wanted nothing more from it

than a little model kit

I told a friend about my plan

with the money safe inside my hand

he'd like to help, he would admit

but he did not have a model kit

I skipped along a country road

like a yearling, young and bold

I came upon a country store

and knocked upon the wooden door

"We've kites, and capes, and needle knits,

and kettles full of candy corn,

but not a single model kit

do we have for you this morn."

I took a trolley to the square

with many shops and people there

but only found to my despair

the shops were closed and the streets were bare

I stood before a river grand

as Darkness chased the day away

opened up my tightened hand

and watched the money fly away

Daniel Dechenaux

THE EDGE OF THE FOREST

I stood before a frightful forest

and gazed at the oaks, so thick and strong

they were like the walls of a medieval fortress

commanding me to go back home

I listened to the sounds from inside of the forest

screaming to me of the dangers inside

with the hooting of owls, the howling of

wolves,

and the hissing of the wind as it burst through

the leaves

I saw lightning flash through the sky

there, then gone, as if turned by a switch

I heard the patter of the falling rain

as from buckets, or barrels, I couldn't say which

Over my shoulder, I glanced at the valley

remembering always from where I have come

I turned and stepped into the forest

Daniel Dechenaux

for only with courage can great things be done

WHAT IF

What if our eyes all saw the same

if we looked not from where we came,

Would we so quickly place the blame

if our eyes all saw the same?

What if our ears would listen, too

if you heard me and I heard you,

I only need to make it through,

am I not a lot like you?

What if our mouths would speak kind words

if praise and thanks were all we heard,

Would it really be absurd

for our mouths to speak kind words?

What if you put your hand in mine

if one by one we formed a line,

Around the world we'd make a chain

if our eyes would see the same

LET HIM SHOWER YOU

Let Him shower you

replacing your sadness with joy

leaving only gladness to shine in your eyes

Let Him shower you

washing away your frustrations

leaving only peace to rest in your heart

Let Him shower you

cleansing away the heat of the world

like a sudden summer storm, leaving you cool

and fresh

Let Him shower you

splashing aside your temptations

like an oasis, satisfying your thirst

Let Him shower you

with His love so strong and His gift so lasting

let Him shower you

Daniel Dechenaux

PEACE INSIDE YOUR HEART

Peace inside your heart

it can come from knowing who you are

may you find exactly who you are

and have peace inside your heart

Feather in the wind

drifting about, and always with a grin

in the end you're sure that you will win

are you a feather in the wind?

Swan upon a pond

swimming around and seldom go beyond

still, you have everything you want

are you a swan upon a pond?

Squirrel up in a tree

counting nuts, as happy as can be

you never know just what winter might bring

are you a squirrel up in a tree?

Daniel Dechenaux

Peace inside your heart

it can come from knowing who you are

may you find exactly who you are

and have peace inside your heart

SECTION FOUR:

SMILE

Daniel Dechenaux

SMILE

Smile 'cause Jesus loves you, anyway

Smile, His love lives on from day to day

If your troubles aren't few

I know what you could do

A smile could help you through

Smile, no matter what the world might bring

Smile, the world is just a passing thing

Yes, your pain will someday end

And Jesus is your friend

So won't you smile, again?

OH WHAT A MIRACLE

Water into wine

Oh, what a miracle!

Water into wine

Oh, what a miracle!

And He made the water into wine

Walk across the sea

Oh, what a miracle!

Walk across the sea

Oh, what a miracle!

And, you know, He walked across the sea

Gave His life for me

Oh, what a miracle!

Gave His life for me

Oh, what a miracle!

And, you know, He gave his life for me

TOGETHER WITH HIM

And so, we will rise,

as if we were balloons escaping from the

hands of a child

into the sky

The tranquil sky,

reuniting us with those for whom we have

cried

joyfully,

Daniel Dechenaux

peacefully,

painlessly,

together with Him

THE FRUITS OF THE LORD

Grapes, hanging on the vines,

we love to squeeze you into wine

we have nothing quite as fine

as you, the grapes onto the vines

Cherries, resting in the trees,

we pull your stems between our teeth

we have nothing quite so sweet

as you, the cherries in the trees

Daniel Dechenaux

Berries, scattered in the woods,

for jams and pies Grandmother cooks

we have nothing quite as good

as you, the berries in the woods

PEANUT BUTTER AND JELLY

How I love to fill my belly

with creamy peanut butter and jelly,

And chocolate milk to wash it down

will make a smile from any frown

Chunky, smooth, thick or thin

whatever way will make me grin,

Apple, grape or marmalade

it doesn't matter how it's made

And when I'm done you may discover

if I'm not full I'll have another,

Because I love to fill my belly

with creamy peanut butter and jelly

MORNINGS FILLED WITH JOY AND

SPLENDOR

Mornings filled with joy and splendor

revealing all He's given me,

January through December

Summer, Autumn, Winter, Spring

Lazy days beside the ocean

Purple leaves beneath the trees

Snowmen standing by my window

A gentle breeze across my cheek

Every day I gain some pleasure

from something He has given me,

And so it's easy to remember

mornings filled with joy and splendor

THE SUNNY SIDE OF THE STREET

On the sunny side of the street

the children sing of peace, not war

as they play by the candy store

On the sunny side of the street

the old men say that prejudice stopped

as they sit by the barber shop

On the sunny side of the street

the waiters speak of love, not hate

down by the pizza place

Won't you walk along with me

on the sunny side of the street?

A LONG WAY TO GO

More hills to climb

no matter how high

More rivers to cross

no matter how wide

More joy to find

no matter how elusive

More possibilities to prove

no matter how impossible

Still, a long way to go

Daniel Dechenaux

A MOTHER IS A GIFT

Like a box on Christmas morning

opened to reveal something special

a mother is appreciated

Like a beautiful balloon

rising high above a green field

a mother lifts your spirits

Like a bridge across the sea

leading you safely to the other side

a mother points you toward your dreams

A mother is a gift from heaven

to love and to cherish

forever

Daniel Dechenaux

LET IN THE SUN

Precious is the time

that we have together

Precious is the love

that we have to share

If we can dream it

we can make it happen

If we open our windows

and…Let in the Sun!

ABOUT THE AUTHOR

This is the author's first compilation of Christian poems.

Printed in the United States
by Baker & Taylor Publisher Services